Practical Management
from Theory to Practice

Stavros Baroutas

To my loving family

About the author

I have written several books about personal development and leadership books printed in Greek and English.

I have studied Marketing at Ulster University and I have acquired my MBA from Kingston University, UK. My next degree was in 2007 a PhD from a US University in Leadership. From June 2016 I am Certified Innermetrix Consultant and few more certifications which it is easily readable from my personal web site www.baroutas.com or from my LinkedIn profile.
In 2009 I was awarded from Chartered Management Institute, UK, as a Chartered Manager (CMgr) in leading people and leading change skills. I am also a members of the Subject Matter Experts Group of Chartered Management Institute.
Throughout my academic studies I have held various posts mainly at pharmaceutical and retail companies where my duties included besides sales, training of employees and directors from basic orientation, emotional intelligence, on the job training and personal development. Furthermore, from January 2003 to February 2007 I personally held consulting and training seminars in sales, management, communication and personal development.
Since December 2008 I am Head of Sales in a big pharmaceutical company. In my free time I teach strategy, leadership, personal development and change management.

For more information visit my personal website
www.baroutas.com

Introduction

I have chosen to be provocative in this book on purpose, and share some of the thoughts and practical knowledge which helped me overcome tricky situations during challenging times. I have tried to put all the study cases mentioned in the book in simple words and I consider them largely realistic, seeing that the tips included come from real-life situations.

The cases I explore in this book do not reduce to a single point in space. Through my attempt to portray an ideal scenario, I aim to demonstrate that such facts occur anywhere in the world, and these are just a few that I have chosen to present you with. Accordingly, the collection of these data reflects my very own path in life and my experience out of the different companies I have served in. I have chosen to present my arguments in a simple and tactile way, avoiding highly tailored language which could baffle readers, or complex theories whose outcomes often contradict them in the first place. Likewise, I have decided not to include a table of contents, as I reckon that this work flows naturally as it is.

In this sense, I am starting this book with the axiom that a manager can also be a leader when circumstances allow. I have expressed the same view in earlier books and I do believe that, whether an individual can be considered a leader or merely a manager is to be determined by how well he or she responds to given circumstances. In today's challenging corporate setting, virtually anyone has the opportunity to climb up the business hierarchy. What you need is insight, strong will and the desire, as well as the opportunity to be distinguished among others. You have a race ahead of you, though there is no baton to be passed to the next runner; it is all about the finishing line.

This book includes 50 tips and ways to implement them so as to benefit from principles which are already widely known. Creativity and different approaches while following people's advice may lead to very different outcomes. It is this difference in approach that distinguishes an individual, as well as the approach itself. In a way, it becomes one's trademark and recipe for success. After all, anyone can be receptive to different tips and ideas, but it is only a few that will actually put these tips into practice, and the ones to succeed are even fewer. As Herb Kelleher of Southeastern Airlines puts it, "we have a strategic plan. It's called doing things."

Execution is the essence then, or, according to General Electric: "Planning is Good, Doing is Better". It is remarkable how much time is wasted by various organisations in planning and preparing for given schemes. This is exactly the reason why I decided to also omit a bibliography session in this book. This work is purely about implementation and execution; management in action.

In order to become a successful team leader, one has to master the basic principles of Management and Leadership. If one is to become a manager, he or she has to study and comprehend Management principles like Planning, Organising, Staffing, Directing and Controlling. Executives who hold a higher position in hierarchy are not necessarily designated to become managers. The way I see it, understanding basic Management principles is essential for an individual's righteous promotion to a senior Management role. Best case scenario would include academic training over Management theories and approaches and, ideally, a skilled director-mentor who will guide individuals over the process of effectively implementing the aforementioned principles.

Nevertheless, training is not enough to make one a successful leader. True leaders must have principles and moral beliefs, a true vision, and most importantly the ability to inspire individuals to support them in their schemes.

The tips suggested in this book are in accordance with the principles mentioned above. However, they cannot be properly applied without a sound knowledge of Management procedures.

I genuinely hope that this book will inspire and be of help to you.

Tip #1

A leader can not and must not merely be a 'theory guru'.

Leaders ought to inspire other people by means of their own attitude. They must appear invulnerable and infallible; modest, and proud; determined to move from words to actions and pave the way for others to follow. In case they notice that people do not conform to given orders, they must be able to judge whether there has been good will on their side, and thus be lenient, or if the issue has been caused by a manager's negligence, and thus be as strict as the circumstances require, at the same time trying to figure what has prevented these individuals from supporting them in the first place. After all, a leader's approach to problematic behaviours is also a fair indicator of what a proper attitude should be.

In case leaders fail to act in line with their own indications, they ought to admit the inconsistency and try to get a 'vote of confidence' all the way from the start. People can not but appreciate the integrity demonstrated by such a gesture.

Nonetheless, leaders who focus in theory and neglect action are leaders who lack vision and stimulation for new ideas. They are incapable of testing new ideas to see how they work and what their outcome will be. Naturally, this reflects to their followers as well. People lose their trust and leaders end up losing the charisma that led them where they are in the first place.

One could take the case of the successful business magnate, Donald Trump, who mainly operates in the field of real estate and has founded the Trump Institute. The aim of Trump Institute is to teach students the secrets of succeeding into the market. What makes Donald Trump a person of great influence is the fact that he first succeeded in his field of endeavour in practice, and he then moved into teaching his enteprenerial approaches in theory.

Tip #2

It is only when you gain a deeper understanding of your own feelings that you will be able to use emotional intelligence as a means to improve communication with others. Up until then, everything lies in theory.

It takes time and effort to be able to understand your feelings and control your emotions. In an attempt to demonstrate the extent of self-restraint people should have, a friend once told me: "never be the one to phrase your thoughts first".

Emotional intelligence can be seen as an outcome of individuals' effort to comprehend their inner self. This is an ever-progressive situation which is nurtured by time and external stimuli. Only after mastering their inner emotions are individuals able to turn theory into action.

Let us examine an incident that happened in Manila, Philippines, which demonstrates how people might fail to understand the importance of emotional intelligence. In one of the businesses which operated in an emerging market, a department supervisor used to make employees work long hours, without ever praising them or showing any sign of appreciation for their hard work. Instead, he used to keep track of all their moves and time all of their breaks. As a consequence, people felt that they were working like slaves and started resigning one after the other.

It was not long before the damage in the department started to show and the supervisor was made redundant. During his final interview to his director and just before he was fired, the supervisor admitted that he never realised he was causing his team members so much distress. This is a typical case of failing to perceive other people's feelings.

"Something that cannot work it's not practical"

Tip #3

In its people aspect, Management has to do with psychology and management of emotions, with the purpose of pushing the workforce towards given objectives.

Given that Human Resources are an indispensable part of Management, high performance depends largely on the team's morale. Impressively high performances and successful business profiles are mostly reported when employees are passionate and excited about work.

According to Jamie Dimon, chief executive officer of JPMorgan Chase, individuals with a high intelligence quotient (IQ) also tend to be the most successful. What he does not take into account, though, is that they might fall short in terms of emotional intelligence (low EQ). The last is an asset to cultivate throughout one's lifetime and it is the foundation of success, as individuals with a high EQ inspire other people through their actions.

Tip #4

Given the circumstances, it might be a good idea to keep your enemies closer. However, it is essential to remember that you will always be on different sides.

It is not uncommon to see business executives with very different philosophies come together for the sake of common goals. Provided that they are not worlds apart, they choose to review their approaches and compromise in an attempt to reach success.

In terms of politics, for instance, this happens when two different parties collaborate for a country's interests and the common good. The same holds for countries that choose to form alliances against a common enemy, as is the case with NATO. As long as the transition is smooth, each of these coalitions is a more powerful formation.

On a business level, an example would be the case of collaboration between two biotechnology companies, Watson Pharmaceuticals and Amgen Pharmaceuticals, for the manufacturing of pharmaceutical products. Watson Pharmaceuticals is a specialty pharmaceutical company that develops, manufactures and distributes generic, brand and biosimilar products, while Amgen is Amgen is the world's largest independent biotechnology firm. Their merger will lead in the manufacturing of biosimilar products, which will pay off for both companies.

Tip #5

It is only after acknowledging change as a principle that one can embrace and fully accept it. This attitude enables individuals to better adjust to ever-changing circumstances.

Given the current dramatic socio-economic changes, if an organisation is to have a prosperous future rather than merely survive, it needs to develop a **positive stance** and a **prompt response** to changing circumstances.

This is, really, the least to be done. In order for an organisation, a business executive, or an entire country to secure their place in today's ever-changing reality, they need to be able to foresee change rather than merely adjusting to it.

Speed is a critical factor here. The quicker an organisation adjusts to changes, the quicker it can move to planning and implementing given schemes.

Many people have seen IMF's intervention in Europe as a positive development for the countries which, economy-wise, got off the track, and believe that its action is essential to save these countries from an economic collapse. Therefore, the sooner these countries accept this new reality and start collaborating, the sooner they will be able to overcome crisis. Ireland is an indicative case here, as it swiftly managed to recover and get back into a healthy financial state.

"The theories are fundamental but we need practice"

In times of high pressure and rapid progress, even the most inspiring values may not survive the passage of time.

Efficient groups which operate under a positive organisational culture do not form in one day. Large companies which invest in the development of their services also pay a lot of attention at the morale of the workplace and aim at developing a strong culture within the company.

In order for a company to keep its appeal, it is necessary to implement the systems, procedures and rituals that will ensure its popularity. Moreover, great care is to be put in procedures which determine the staff's attitude and the customers' perception.

Companies should be found on the basis of principles which will ensure that they have support during the challenging stage of their development. Such principles should be well-defined, highly realistic and inspired by given leaders. As mentioned earlier, they should define the organisation and contribute to the development of its culture. For instance, when a company is making its first steps in the market, these principles should provide a response to such questions as "who are we?" and "what are we here to do?". Besides, leaders' role is crucial here, as they ought to promote these principles and cultivate them, in collaboration with the rest of their business associates.

Curt Anastasio, President and CEO of NuStar Energy L.P. is a typical case of a leader who is constantly trying to instill the strategy and vision of the company in his associates, as well as teach them the proper mode of thinking and acting. Through the relationship he builds with his associates, he is able to comprehend their problems and provide rapid solutions. Bonding with his executives also constitutes his motto, as for him employee safety is a top priority. It is worth highlighting that, even thought the company is making remarkable and rapid progress, company values remained the same.

It goes without saying that one should never stop investing in values, not only within a company but also on a broader context.

Tip #7

Leaders must be able to form balanced relationships with people around them and always be innovative in their actions.

In order for a group or organisation to be successful, it should operate on the basis of such principles as justice, equality and impartiality. These allow leaders to proceed with innovative action, at the same time keeping the balance within the company. The notion of balance here is used in the sense of a harmonious cooperation within different executives and work groups.

In this way, leaders are capable of charting a course for the future of the organisation and secure their place in it. At the same time, they should also be ready to risk their own place if they are to keep the harmony within the workplace.

Marissa Mayer, President and CEO of Yahoo, argues that the best way to make decisions which are favourable for a company's future is through communication and collaboration in such contexts as coffee places, corridors and meeting rooms. This way, colleagues get to bond at an emotional and psychological level.
All things considered, leaders play a crucial role in fostering favourable circumstances and addressing conflicts between executives in the workplace.

Tip #8

In order to achieve your goals, just close your eyes and think: What is it that you really want to achieve? Are there any features in your approach that you could improve? Stop looking for answers in the wrong places and allow yourself the time to think these questions through. Once you define your goal, do everything in your powers to achieve it.

An organisation's distinction in its field of endeavour comes with successful performance and high abilities. First step is to determine one's choice and focus, then employ sound judgement, and eventually proceed to action and final success.

Jeff Bezos, for example, knew exactly what he wanted, and that was to transform Amazon online merchant of books into one of the largest online enterprises. He was able to predict and identify buyers' wishes before they logged off his online webpage. He aimed at rendering his small-scale business into a colossal online enterprise and this is exactly what he did.

"A leader, who is not a practitioner, he is just an ideologist"

Tip #9

Always keep in mind that there is no such thing as an ideal approach.

Managers and leaders act according to what they consider the best option, taking into account given circumstances. Naturally, the setting in modern societies changes swiftly. As a consequence, it so happens that managers/leaders who have been very competent at some point, are not achieving the same results under different circumstances, regardless of what their actual skills are. Indeed, skills are of much importance and hard times call for improved competencies. However, it is important to keep in mind that leaders are only humans. There is always room for errors and it is from these errors that leaders learn and manage to grow. Therefore, among leaders' foremost duties is to deal with given circumstances in the best possible way and act for the benefit of their supporters.

Having established that, one might think of Steve Jobs, whose rigid management tactics, radical economic views and firm attitude with employees led to a conflict on 1985 with John Sculley, who was at the time CEO of Pepsi, and ended up in his seclusion and final withdrawal from the company. His return in Apple a decade later is considered of major importance for the company's survival. Within just a few years and through a series of steps for revisiting the structures of its departments and products, such as discarding Apple Newton, merging all Macintosh models in two series, ensuring a 100 million dollars investment from Microsoft and contracting with them for the continuous support of Macintosh platform for 5 years, Apple manages to stand on its feet again and start making profit.

The outcome leads us to the initial observation a few lines above: Once circumstances changed, once redundant Steve Jobs was deemed as indispensable for Apple.

Tip #10

The best thing to do when met with unfortunate circumstances is to employ good old humour. It is often very stressful for managers to keep everything under control. In times like these, a touch of humour is enough to get anyone "back in the game".

Rule number 1 when met with unfortunate circumstances is to try to save some valuable time. It is a good idea to shift the conversation to some other argument in case this has a positive effect. You would never imagine how much you could achieve with just a witty line or an insightful remark. After all, nothing can boost your confidence more and help you fight stress better than a smile from your interlocutor and a sign that your attempt to compromise things has been successful.

For instance, Ben Who, CEO of a mass media company, is determined that humour is a crucial part of his successful career so far. Therefore, he did not hesitate to take part in a reality show which satirises an employee's life in his own company.

Humour helps to enliven a monotonous office environment, reduces stress and motivates employees to become proactive and innovative. Particularly in times of crisis, humour helps to bring things back to normal and gives employees a sense of hope.

"We need to have a "how to do this" procedure in our minds"

Tip #11

In times of crisis, leaders must be able to give their supporters hope.

Team leaders should always have a vision for their team members, as well as themselves. When things go wrong, it is this vision that keeps the hope alive. The ability to inspire and give hope to people is a fair indicator of leaders' skills.

Naturally, not all leaders are equally gifted. It might be the case that circumstances are not fostering a leader's vision or do not render the need for hope as clear as it should be. In any case, the stronger the leaders' vision, the more powerful their influence and message of hope to their supporters. Leaders can also refer to encouraging examples from everyday life in order to strengthen their arguments.

In an event hosted by Olitechs Ltd, Phil Wall of HopeHIV spoke about the organisation's contribution to protecting orphans in Africa. He highlighted the importance of individuals' involvement in the organisation and the difference it has made to people in need of support in Africa. Through his inspirational speech, he managed to give the audience hope for a better future.

Write down what you are thinking

Tip #12

Stress often prevents individuals from responding to given circumstances. On the other hard, it might also contribute to personal progress and improvement. In any case, individuals must not allow stress to interfere with their ability to think clearly.

During highly stressful times, anyone can freeze up or make the wrong decision. It is in times like these where people tend to lose control. First thing to do in such cases is to acknowledge the situation and take a break. People need some time to regain self-control before they are able to take matters into their own hands again.

Stress may also be related to fear for particular circumstances. Again, one has to follow the same course of action. First step is to put things on hold, then think things over, and finally act in order to regain self-control.

Research shows that approximately one-quarter of the employees surveyed consider their job the number one factor causing stress in their lives (Nortwestern National Life). Likewise, ¾ of the employees surveyed believe that their generation experiences more stress in the workplace than previous generations (Princeton Survey research Associates). Finally, it appears that employees are more likely to allow health issues to interfere with their normal working conditions, rather than financial or personal concerns.

Tip #13

Self-improvement goes hand in hand with questioning modern reality. In other words, critical thinking is crucial for personal progress.

These might all sound irrelevant or even impossible. However, it is the act of questioning circumstances alone which triggers alertness, challenges current reality, encourages innovative thinking and leads to original ideas. Naturally, new thoughts and ideas are filtered by critical thinking. Sound judgement is necessary for perceiving and interpreting reality in a novel way. After all, our brain is just like any other muscle in our body. Lack of practice leads to atrophy and eventually results in idleness.

In a survey carried out by IBM and involving 1709 CEOs from around the world, 75% of the individuals questioned replied that effective collaboration leads to growth. Another 67% replied that it promotes communication, and a 61% reckoned that it encourages flexible and creative thinking. The above scores highlight the importance of individuals' ability to progress, at the same time spreading the knowledge to the rest of the employees, thus also promoting collaboration and effective communication.

"Today in times of crisis we need practice more than ever to reform our organizations"

Tip #14

Sometimes people ask themselves questions like: "Why did this have to happen to me?"
Just think of how much more beneficial it would be to think over what choices might have brought them in that situation.

It so happens that in times of high pressure and stress, we all find ourselves in that position and we all wonder why some things had to happen to us. Each of us manages to overcome unfortunate circumstances according to how well we adjust to them and resume action under different settings. Also important is one's ability to see things under a different perspective and respond promptly to unexpected circumstances.

One could suggest that this was indeed a challenge for former president of the United States, George W. Bush, after September 11, 2001 terrorist attacks in the World Trade Centre complex in New York City. The policies adopted by him and his predecessors reinforced the anti-American sentiment and led to the establishment of terrorist organisations within the Islamic world. Despite their claims, none of them where able to predict the turn of events and prepare for the consequences to follow.

Tip #15

Friendships within the workplace are a source of motivation during stressful times.

Bonding of employees leads to a pleasant atmosphere in the workplace and promotes trust among colleagues. In this way, everyone works in unison for the common good of the company and the achievement of common goals. At the same time, and given that everyone is making the same effort towards the realisation of the company's vision, employees in the workplace manage to toss formalities aside and develop a closer relationship.

In effect, most part of training in US companies takes place in as informal settings as office corridors, or even in situations occurring out of the workplace context. This way, employees improve their ability to communicate and engage in fruitful cooperation. In this context, the terms 'friend' and 'colleague' complement each other for the sake of interest and success.

Susan Stevenson, CEO at CIGNA healthcare company in Hong Kong, used to call everyone in the workplace with their first name and she aimed at organising out of office events, thereby encouraging employees to bond and form more meaningful relationships.

Moreover, irrespective of her high position in hierarchy, she was open to suggestions from everyone within the company, a fact which highlights her modesty. One can read more about her in an article featuring in the University of Southern California website and titled: "My Favorite CEO; Susan Stevenson".

"A leader / manager needs knowledge, passion and practical thinking to be effective"

Tip #16

Change is partly dictated by what individuals choose to focus on.

Indeed, change is the only option during challenging times when societies keep transforming according to constant migration, given taxation policies, accessibility [or not] to education, corrupted governments, company mergers or bankruptcy, and a globalisation model which is largely considered to be unsuccessful. In times like these, change is dictated by market and competition terms but it is often hard for individuals to accept and embrace it.

However, the need to improve one's skills in order to respond to changing circumstances is not merely dictated by business concerns, but it is also essential in personal and family life. Otherwise, societies are unavoidably met with insecurity, high pressure and the need to manage the consequences of change. In any case, individuals will only be able to embrace change once they acknowledge the new reality and accept to become a part of it.

The above are also cited in my book titled *Change; a choice to determine success.*

Change is a secret weapon and the key to success when one's rivals are unwilling to risk choosing a different path and being innovative. It is also worth mentioning the extent to which the workforce is willing to change established attitudes routines and staff hours, or even a compromise in their earnings for as long as the transition lasts. After all, everyone should be able to compromise and be more tolerant during challenging times.

Jørgen Vig Knudstorp, current CEO of the Lego Group, assumed office in a time when the company was on the verge of collapse, but gradually managed to change it into a successful business all over again. This took a shift in the way the company approached the market so far, at the same time rendering organisational structure stricter, particularly regarding supervisors and decision-making in lower levels of hierarchy.

Tip #17

Effective communication is crucial in achieving change step by step. Sound relationships and effective collaboration within the workplace are highly important for the establishment of a politically correct work environment. It is also essential that change is managed by a skilful leader who dares to be honest with people.

Therefore, it is the responsibility of highest executives to establish effective communication terms within the company and maintain them when it comes to customers, suppliers and employees. Naturally, employees must always be agreeable with customers and company suppliers.

When it comes to Greece, the above are subject to a significant risk, which is no other than hierarchy bypass. Relationships and good communication within the workplace are to be encouraged under the condition that each individual has a specific ranking in the hierarchy and is not meant to deviate from it. What is meant by this is essentially that everyone needs to do their job in the best of their capacities, at the same time respecting the hierarchy balance and minding not to expose themselves with their actions.

In this respect, WD-40's CEO managed to make his company a well-oiled machine by establishing certain terms and conditions. Through this approach, and by giving them more responsibilities, he aimed at showing employees that the directors truly value their contribution to the company. Indeed, employees felt that their efforts are acknowledged and thus demonstrated improved performance.

"Theory + practice =
new ways of thinking and perhaps new theories"

Tip #18

When planning to implement change, always keep an eye on the budget.

Changes take time and money, particularly when it comes to organisational schemes and transformations. Hence, a company should always take the factor of change into account and thus reserve part of the budget for respective circumstances. However, lower cost expenses, such as the ones necessary for training employees and providing for their needs during working hours, should also be taken under consideration.

For instance, the HR department in Zappos employs a team whose task is to carry the message of the company to employees and teach them the established policies and values. Despite the high cost of forthcoming change, the company does not fail to invest time and money in preparing the workforce for the new business reality.

Tip #19

Leaders cannot implement change successfully unless they ensure the support of their people.

Managers must be devoted to their tasks and put their best efforts towards rendering the new business terms effective. If only the new business schemes are to be successful, managers ought to avoid prejudice and favouritism.

However, there is a limit to what leaders are able to achieve in their own right. Therefore, they always need a team to support their ideas, strategy and vision. On the other hand, followers need to adopt these values themselves in order to be able to practice them for the interest of the company. In other words, managers are invaluable to a leader. This presupposes that they act in complete accordance with the leader's principles and company overview. In turn, the leader must be impartial and unbiased, and maintain the feeling of justice even in the most challenging situations.

Robert LoCascio, CEO of LivePerson, wanted to change the culture within his company. In order to achieve that, he asked the employees to take part in a survey related to the establishment of values which best convey the vision of the company. The survey came down to two main principles only: be your own master and be helpful to others. Employees' devotion to these principles was unanimous for the simple reason that they had a say in determining them, therefore they truly represented their views about the company.

Write down what you are thinking

Tip #20

Even superman had to learn how to fly first!

Higher executives often expect too much from employees in lower positions, without providing them with any guidelines or former training for any of the tasks required. This usually happens during extremely busy periods when executives do not have enough time to provide adequate training. However, it is often the case that individuals who have had little to no formal training manage to execute tasks with the utmost efficiency.

In highly stressful working periods, not only do supervisors often have unrealistic demands, but they also need everything done 'yesterday'. These situations call for employees' own initiative and personal judgement. Naturally, no one can guarantee the outcome of such 'on the spot' decisions, as each individual acts on the basis of personal skills and experience. Hence, it's up to the supervisor to either praise employees' proactiveness, or judge their decisions according to their own experience.

Professional investor, Benjamin Graham, taught business magnate and investor, Warren Buffet, when the last was a student at Columbia Business School. Benjamin Graham is considered the father of value investing. He was the one to teach young Warren Buffet how to successfully make his way through the investment world. As a result, Buffet is now one of the richest people in the world.

"Realize the on-going procedure means transforming things with reality"

Tip #21

During unfortunate circumstances like the economic crisis we are currently facing, it is crucial to focus on the outcome, as this might as well define the future of an organisation.

Given the distress in the global financial system, organisations must follow strategies which minimise risks and aim at the best possible financial outcome.

Likewise, long-term contracts or agreements with external clients during recession are not cost-effective. However, economic crisis is often favourable in terms of making solid agreements and thus eliminating the chances of failure. It is advisable to renegotiate on terms agreed with clients at least once a year.

A very important development for the future of the Greek defence industry is the participation of the Greek company METKA in the production of battle tanks Leopard 2 for Qatar. METKA is commissioned by Germany's Krauss Maffei Wegmann (KMW) to construct the armoured hulls and towers for 62 Leopard 2 tanks. The 56.5 million euros agreement is expected to be signed soon, it includes little to no risk, and it will bring considerable profit to METKA, at the same time ensuring plenty of new job openings. The outcome in this case, is no other than the survival of the organisation against the challenging financial times.

Tip #22

Now is the time to become indispensable to your company.

People in the past used to believe in the axiom that nobody is irreplaceable. Today, though, employees who achieve high performance and ensure high profits, at the same time respecting the policy of the company, are indeed indispensable.

Steven Paul Jobs, former chairman and CEO of Apple Inc. is widely recognised as a charismatic pioneer of the personal computer revolution. After a power struggle with the board of directors in 1985, Jobs left Apple and founded the computer platform development company NeXT. Apple then went through a stage which was critical for its survival. Jobs returned to Apple in 1996 and within a few years, he managed to turn it into a top-notch technology company. Hence, he became indispensable.

"After all, you need the right people to execute your idea"

Tip #23

From small groups to entire companies, cohesion is a vital element for success.

Cohesion is a prerequisite for the harmonious operations and the achievement of the goals of any company. Coherent teams are able to perform efficiently, and have a direct approach to problem solution and task execution. Within coherent teams there is always noble competition and passion for their field of endeavour and their company.

"One Microsoft all the time" is Microsoft Corporation's motto, calling for "one strategy, united together, with great communication, decisiveness and positive energy". All departments cooperate efficiently towards manufacturing software products, which are the main source of income for the company.

At the same time, offering high quality services is at the heart of Microsoft. The company aims at promoting the message of cohesion and introducing a familiar environment into the market.

In effect, the company was structured according to the field of endeavour of each department, whether this is Marketing, Engineering, and so on. Hence, all departments work in accordance with the company's policies.

Tip #24

4 *essential steps to becoming a great leader: work hard, be brave, care about your followers, care about your company (or country).*

These might sound too simplistic, however in practice, not only are they hard to achieve, but it is also rare to find them all in one person. Indeed, it is hard to find a leader who ticks all the boxes and at the same time has a clear vision and judgement.

It is the extend to which leaders fulfil these requirements that makes followers support them in their future schemes. This can only be true if leaders prove that they work hard to stay true to their values and commitments, not hesitating to engage in arguments and negotiations in order to prove with words and actions that they genuinely care about their followers. 'Commitment' here, refers to dedication to other people's problems and making their resolution a priority.

Rule number 4 suggests that leaders must love their company, organisation or country, in case we refer to a political figure. Yet, one has to agree that during the past few years we are seriously lacking such leading figures and there is, thus, an explicit need for gifted individuals with solid management and leadership skills.

A typical case of an inspiring leader is Cuba's political leader, Fidel Castro. Armed with his revolutionary ideas and the love and support of his followers, he fights for the rights of his country against the global forces that claim Cuba's resources.

In times of crisis, the answer lies in assertive leadership.

For years and years people used to live in prosperous societies, ignoring rules, accomplishing all of their needs and thus forming a mentality which is totally different to today's reality.

Nowadays, heavy taxation, the crisis of small and medium-sized enterprises and the constant financial pressure in the public sector create unfavourable circumstances, unlike the ones people were used to in the past. Employees who have not realised the current state of affairs may inhibit the progress within a company.

Be that as it may, I do not support the view that such employees should be made redundant. What I mean here is that, insofar as they do not realise the importance of the current situation, they halt the company's progress towards a point where bankruptcy is no longer an imminent risk.

Under the circumstances, it may be necessary that leaders make their followers execute certain tasks when these are essential for the progress of the organisation.

Douglas County-based Dish Network has been branded as the worst company to work for in America during the severe crisis of 2012. According to Bloomberg, the company's chairman, Charlie Ergen, is responsible for this labelling, due to the high pressure and severity he exerts to the employees. At the same time, he is also claimed to be responsible for the company's successful course.

"Management is a combination of different fields of study; psychology, marketing, communication, biology, creativity"

Tip #26

Now is the time to become a hero.

The economic crisis of 2009 sparked the creation of an "encryption-based society". It affected the delicate balance of the society and enterprises and enabled entrepreneurs and managers in all fields to develop skills, seize opportunities and often stretch to their limits for the sake of their organisations, most of the time with nothing to gain in return.

It follows that people had to respond to the new circumstances and make progress in all fronts so as to be able to survive. Individuals who manage to get distinguished for their skills, employing ethical means and caring for fellow citizens, may as well be called the heroes of our times.

Our case study here is 'Mr. Jumbo', Apostolos Vakakis, a leading figure in the Greek retail trade, who runs one of the the most profitable businesses in the Greek market. He has managed to distinguish himself as a success case study by introducing cheap toys and accessories to the market and advertising in a creative and humorous way. He dared to take risks during uncertain times and soon became a prominent figure in Greek business.

Naturally, I do not mean to suggest that Apostolos Vakakis is a hero, as I do not know the circumstances that led him to where he is today. Nevertheless, one has to agree that he is a leader in his field of endeavour. The same holds for all the entrepreneurs who cautiously calculate their daily earnings, at the same time minimising costs as much as possible and hoping that their instinct will lead them to the right decisions.

Crisis and unfortunate circumstances create an interesting contrast when it comes to leadership. While it can be easier for leaders to distinguish themselves from the crowd, at the same time it is hard to make the right decisions as to leadership approaches and strategies.

In times of crisis, few people dare to take initiatives. As a consequence, competition is lower and that makes it easier for someone to distinguish among others. Hence, individuals who aspire to hold leadership positions manage to prove their determination for success and thus earn people's trust.

The solution lies in unique leadership approaches.

Like so, Former CEO of AlphaGraphics, Kevin Cushing, took the initiative to work with franchisers, despite the risk of having to reconcile his company's vision with different views of businessmen who aspire to set their own businesses. This turned out to be a profitable strategy for AlphaGraphics and it would not have been implemented if it was not for Kevin Cushing and his skilful team.

"You just imagine yourself implementing the idea, step by step"

Tip #28

'Exiting from crisis' policies are implemented by leaders who admittedly failed to rise up to the circumstances and only attempted to avoid the tragic implications after they have already led their countries towards it.

The contrast here lies in the fact that, while these leaders keep adopting severe measures in order to relieve their countries' financial burden and lower their debt, they bear a significant part of the responsibility for the current situation.

It follows, that these leaders also largely contributed to the establishment of current socio-political climate. Likewise, they had a part in electing other leaders too, so it is their kind of people who take all sorts of decisions for the country today.

To make matters worse, they will turn out to be harmful for their country's future for yet another reason: their decisions are short-sighted and they won't do us any good in the long run. On the contrary, they will incur even higher levels of unemployment, further cuts to salaries and wages, as well as another increase in the retirement age. All these actions, to name a few, render these leaders inefficient. Their vision is a failure, their strategies and negotiation skills are poor.

A typical example can be traced in the generation of the former prime minister of Greece, George Papandreou. Similarly, one can think of leaders who served within the 5 years following 2005, such as Nicolas Sarkozy, George W. Bush, and Silvio Berlusconi, whose unfortunate decisions led their countries to economic depression, poverty and unemployment. What they all did was to protect the already afflicted public sector and come down hard on the private sector where cash flow was already an open wound.

Tip #29

There is a second, 'hidden self' in most individuals. If you already know yours, try to improve it. If not, then now is the time to discover it.

It takes a great deal of courage to put one's self at risk for the common good and this is one of the biggest challenges towards self-improvement.

It is also hard to develop the ability of empathising with others. It takes great skills to be able to discern someone's hidden self and it is necessary to try and improve your 'reading' skills. Once you master this, use your newly acquired skills to help others improve.

Self-sabotaging behavior results from a misguided attempt to rescue ourselves from our own negative feelings.

Chequed.com Founder and CEO, Greg Moran, argues that this hidden self is largely responsible for the wrong choice of associates, thus having a negative impact for the goals of the company and the culture within the workplace. This is an ill-disposed aspect of your hidden self that you are responsible for discovering and enhancing.

"A practitioner looks the picture piece by piece and then makes the appropriate changes"

Tip #30

Sometimes, leaders must follow their own instinct despite what others think. People will call them arrogant; then again, this ought to be the case for a leader.

While this might be true, leaders must also be receptive. Different opinions can shape a leader's perception of facts, thereby facilitating decision making. Nonetheless, time pressure does not always allow room for this.

On the other hand, you may find yourself in a situation where a decision is so hard to make that no-one is willing to help you or show you the right way. In times like these, you have the chance to be a true leader, bear the responsibility of your own decisions and strike out on your own. It is highly likely that your followers will be startled by your moral strength, as well as relieved that they do not share the burden of having to be part of such a hard decision they probably never thought they could take.

Moreover, leaders might act in ways that seem to have little to no short-term impact, but which can turn out to bring their teams to the centre of attention in the long run.

What is more, if you keep conforming to what other people believe every time you are about to take a new step forward of make a new decision, you will either fail or stay in the same situation forever. Unfortunately, other people's views more often than not act as a deterrent to personal initiative, at least to my mind.

Visionary leaders are not born every day. You might be wondering why. Try to liberate your spirit and follow your own instincts. After all, leaders are driven by a sheer will to achieve what they aspire for. It is this passion that attracts followers and makes them support given leaders.

Are you really ready to become a leader? After all, leadership is largely a matter of personal choice.

In order to take Kvaerner ASA back on to the winner's podium, CEO, Mark Toner had to change the organisational culture of the company, lower expenses and remove certain unproductive executives. Even though his decisions were met with objections by some of his colleagues, he did not hesitate to stick to his own strategy and follow his own instinct.

Write down what you are thinking

_____

_____

_____

_____

_____

_____

_____

_____

_____

_____

_____

_____

_____

_____

_____

_____

_____

_____

_____

_____

_____

_____

_____

_____

_____

_____

_____

_____

_____

Tip #31

Always act on the basis of the principles of honesty, freedom of thought, respect and integrity. There is a significant lack of such values in today's societies.

Leaders should try their best to be as flawless as possible. However, this is not possible unless the principles stated above are an integral part of their everyday life. Naturally, leaders can not expect their partners to be honest if they are not being honest themselves in the first place. Dishonest leaders will neither gain their followers' trust nor spread the right messages and values.

Henry McKinnell, former CEO of the board of directors of Pfizer Inc., argues that in order to gain the support of employees, a leader must have an objective attitude, be receptive to their needs and ideas and always stay positive.

Tip #32

Always consider that fatigue can have an impact in your attitude and decisions.

Leaders should always take advantage of their free time to exercise their body and mind. In case this is not possible, they must be twice as careful about their words and actions and remain self-composed. Otherwise, they might end up drawing the wrong conclusions or overreacting when their partners mismanage a situation, when they should be there to support their people in times of heavy stress and fatigue.

An article in Forbes magazine suggests that, in order to beat fatigue in the workplace, we should adopt healthy eating habits, sleep more hours, exercise, consult specialist psychologists and undergo regular health tests.

"Thinking out of the box means to make implementation a great idea"

Tip #33

Sometimes the way you market success is more important than success in the first place.

In this respect, skilful performance alone is not enough, but employees must rather be able to supply written performance reports to their higher executives. After all, "Verba volant, scripta manent"; "spoken words fly away, written words remain".
However, this form of documentation requires attention to certain points.

As the article suggest, the proper and advisable way to present your work to your line managers or directors is to construct reports. This gives you the opportunity to promote yourself as a proactive employee and enhance your performance in the workplace. This way, you will indeed distinguish yourself from the rest of the employees who might consider reports a mere nuisance. At the same time, you invest in your relationship with higher executives by demonstrating the steps you take towards achieving desired goals.

Tip #34

Managers and leaders ought to entertain a group of workers who are not afraid to voice their opinions.

There is no room for fear and prejudice within a work team. Freedom of speech encourages innovation, reinforces cohesion and bonds between colleagues and renders the workforce more productive and efficient. At the same time, it also prevents any underlying intentions and helps resolve problematic situations more swiftly.

In effect, a survey conducted by the Australian union among executives of all levels regarding the issue of ethics in the workplace led to the conclusion that freedom of speech in the workplace is desirable as long as the employees involved make reasonable use of this powerful right.

Tip #35

The tendency to postpone or overcomplicate situations often deters prompt and efficient action.

In order to succeed in one's aspirations, it is necessary to first have a scheme of action and take into account any possible consequences. Action alone can beat procrastination. One just needs to be insightful in order to accurately calculate the next steps and avoid possible risks. At the end of the day, the responsibility must solely be yours.

Tesla Motors, Inc. is an American company that designs, manufactures and sells electric cars and electric vehicle power train components to compete with such manufacturers as Porsche and Ferrari. The company's plan was to make its way into the market by selling to individuals who can afford electric cars, and once it gains enough followers, lower prices to compete with Porsche and Ferrari.

Despite several objections as to the high risks involved in such a scheme of action, the company's CEO, Elon Musk, followed the initial plan and thus managed to render the company a typical case   study   for   success.

"Today to be practical is a challenge"

Tip #36

Lack of experience, insecurity and fear are only some of the factors which prevent us from acting promptly, if at all.

Don't be afraid to make decisions. Remember that experience is often gained through taking risks. The more you try and succeed the more confident you will feel about taking new steps. Therefore, stop sabotaging your own self. Remember that you are here today because of your own achievements. Make use of your acquired skills and talents and act wisely.

William David Perez was made redundant from NIKE during the first month of his employment. The co-founder and chairman of Nike, Inc., Philip Knight, decided to remove him from the company on the grounds that his lack of experience and confidence was affecting his performance. According to Knight, Perez was unable to take matters into his own hands because the requirements in S.C.Johnson & Son Inc. where he used to work are very different from the ones in the area of sports equipment. This decision was met with the support of the company's stakeholders.

Tip #37

A well-thought-out scheme of action can push you to your next career level in the same way as a reckless attitude can have devastating effects.

Beware! It is make or break.

Acting for the sake of action without careful planning might prove to be fruitful for a while, however things will soon fall in digression and the situation might not be reversible. You will soon be met with the consequences of your own actions. This will not only affect other people's trust in you, but most importantly also your confidence about your own skills, which is essential if you aspire to become a leader.

Former J.C. Penney CEO, Ron Johnson, made 4 crucial mistakes which gradually led his company to the wrong direction:
He failed to identify the consumers' needs, he did not test his ideas with clients to see if his practices are acceptable before opening to the market, he restructured the company in a way that did not reflect its original vision and finally he gave his superiors the impression that he lacked respect for the company.

Contribution in management is:
- ✓ **New ideas**
- ✓ **Old ideas with new ways**
- ✓ **Seeing things from another point of view**
- ✓ **Making things works**

AND

RESULTS

Tip #38

You must be accurate and confident about your next steps, rather than being arrogant.

Your decisions and your actions must be conscious so as to allow you to have control of the outcome. In this sense, always try to be one step ahead and be prepared to accept the consequences of your actions. Have faith in your own skills and do not be afraid to show what you are worth. At the same time, be your own self's worst critic. Finally, be modest; yet, do not be humble. Learn to differentiate between self-esteem and arrogance.

On the 15th of May 2013 and during the last two weeks prior to the effective date of capital increase, the National Bank of Greece would have to be recapitalised, after the plan for a merger with Eurobank Ergasias SA (EUROB) was put on hold. However, CEO, Alexandros G. Tourkolias, was able to surmount this obstacle and raise the set funds necessary to keep the bank under the Greek state ownership. Contrary to global market predictions, he was able to approach Greek private investors and businesses and ensure private-sector participation, thus achieving remarkable results.

Tip #39

Vision in terms of leadership is a mixture of reality and leaders' ability to envisage the future.

Leaders must be able to adjust their schemes to given circumstances and be both realists and visionary. This might sound easy in theory, but think of how challenging reality can be with current competition levels and the lack of liquidity.

James D. Sinegal, co-founder and former CEO of Costco, was aiming at selling high volumes of a small variety of goods of the same quality as branded products, at supposedly 'wholesale'-level-low prices. 594 stores later, Costco Wholesale is an international powerhouse that is, as of 2012, the seventh-largest retailer in the world. Sinegal had already stated his vision from 1983 when he took leadership of the company, and he is expanding at an increasing rate during the past 15 years, having the wholehearted support of his colleagues and employees.

"Heroic leadership is leadership in practice with passion"

Tip #40

Leaders ought to exert their power up to a certain extent, even if this breaks the employees' usual routine.

Leaders are expected to be able to 'read' individuals' skills and talents, even the ones that they do not distinguish themselves. Therefore, they must often be demanding so as to get the best out of their employees and help them succeed their goals, each to their own peak of potential.

However, this attitude might be greeted with scepticism and protests among the employees who are likely to be disturbed by this change of scenery. In any case, if employees are unable to realise that certain projects aim at enhancing their performance, then the leader might not need to explain further. He or she has to put pressure for the sake of progress.

Employees who resist change belong to a certain category of individuals who are so used to the status quo that they always have an excuse in place whenever circumstances do not favour them, always excluding themselves from any share of responsibility.

Lori Beth Garver, former Deputy Administrator of NASA, was placed out of the blue in a whole new environment, largely dominated by men, where she had to stretch to her limits, take risks and stand for her arguments.
The challenge was to convince everyone to accept and implement her decisions. By succeeding in that, she managed to put herself in a better position within the NASA society.

Tip #41

Climbing the hierarchy ladder comes with increased responsibilities, more employees to supervise and a more intense work pace which often becomes frenetic.

In times like this, it is essential to have a high degree of self-control. Do not proceed to hasty decisions which you might regret afterwards. If you realise that you are still finding it hard to keep the situation under control, then you might be in need of self-improvement.

Advancing in hierarchy calls for a high level of patience and tolerance for the rest of the employees' mistakes. Some people put it as graphically as having to keep a sip of water in one's mouth up to 30 seconds before being able to think and make decisions in a clear state of mind.

James H. Quigley, CEO of Deloite, argues that only when you treat your partners with respect you are an efficient member of the team with the chance to be accepted as a leader and inspire an enhanced company performance.

Write down what you are thinking

Tip #42

Knowledge is essential in order to be able to interpret the present conditions and foresee future developments.

Leaders must be able to distinguish between real and fake 'prophets'. With 'prophets', I mean individuals whom you can trust and study so as to prepare your response to forthcoming change within the framework of a company of the society.

What is also vital is to be able to handle information without getting lost in a plethora of news which can block your system, upset you and make you waste your time. What you should do is separate the useful from the trivial information by means of thorough examination and discussion with reliable sources.

What is more, do not rush into sharing information for which you are not 100% certain. While information can help you broaden your world-view and shape your own view of reality, if misused, it can tarnish your reputation and spoil the image of you and your company.

Let's take the example of price formation in the stock market. When a financial analyst or investor receives information about the financial state of a company, he or she has to cross-examine and confirm it before proceeding with investments. Naturally, any wrong decisions will lead to financial loss. Such was the case of Lehman Brothers Holdings Inc. which, even though graded as a financially viable company, ended up in a financial ruin, dragging all of its investors down with it.

"Best in class,
- ✓ **Visionary**
- ✓ **Inspiring**
- ✓ **Practical"**

Tip #43

Figures are crucial in times of crisis.

Business executives are expected to ensure high profits and remarkable work for their companies. It is often the case that costly investments push expenses too high and have a disastrous effect for companies. Therefore, costs must be controlled and kept to a minimum.

As a result of the crisis, banks have had to undergo a restructuring of their basic working mechanisms, cutting costs as much as possible in order to survive. This led to smaller branches having to withhold their activity, cut expenses and make employees redundant. The final aim was to reduce the quantitative capital ratio, or, in other words, retain liquidity so as to manage to survive.

Tip #44

Leaders must care for their people.

This translates to being fair to everyone in the company, protecting their interests and ensuring them a prosperous future, irrespective of what they believe it is best for them.

An even more challenging goal is to aspire to make everyone better in what they are doing.

Despite recession, E.J. PAPADOPOULOS S.A., which is primarily known for its food products (biscuits), has managed to gradually increase its profits and re-invest them successfully, hiring new staff, respecting past contracts and ensuring bonuses and allowances according to employees' financial situation.

"My main concern is to offer high quality products, hire new people instead of pushing them away, making planned profits and wise investments", argues CEO and Managing Director at E.J. PAPADOPOULOS SA, Ioanna Papadopoulou, who was awarded the Exceptional Manager 2011 award of excellency.

Tip #45

Mind your own errors.

You are not supposed to make serious mistakes at this stage. To err might be human but this does not necessarily mean that it is acceptable as well. Try not to be influenced by decisions which are not your very own. Spontaneity might as well be a drawback in this context, whereas restraint can be a virtue.

By saying that, I do not mean to suggest that you can never make mistakes. However, make sure they have as little impact as possible and always try to find a way to reverse the situation.

Shape your own idea of the market and use it as a filter to judge given circumstances. The same can apply to your personal affairs.

An article in the paper Usatoday, titled "Learn from your mistakes, then get back to work", suggests that the best way to avoid mistakes is to not let them consume you, be honest, work your alternatives in advance and concentrate on your positive traits.

"Business is a serious game, that's why you must win"

Moreover...

Moving closer to the end, it is about time I revealed the secret recipe for successful and efficient management.

Naturally, I do not mean to underestimate the importance of all the tips suggested up to this point. All of these tips are closely related to everyday life and the critical times we are currently experiencing.

However, I have reserved for the end some principles which I consider the foundation of sound leadership, in other words the essentials for this exciting journey. I am confident that, judging from the below, you will be able to distinguish the individuals who suits your company's profile and can generate the best results.

Tip #46

Do not disclose your thoughts to any of your colleagues.

Delicate issues, rumours, office gossip; keep your thoughts about all these to yourself and make sure you do not spread any 'news' around the workplace. Sometimes people just can not keep things to themselves or do not know how to manage secrets. Issues which seem trivial may as well disrupt the delicate balance and harmony within the workplace, thereby also unsettling the harmonious operations of work teams. Therefore, turning a deaf ear to gossip helps you boost your credibility at work and gain the respect of your peers. Aren't these among your foremost goals in the first place?

Tip #47

Do not disclose company-related issues.

Being aware of "confidential" information means that you might have had the privilege of knowing these but by no means are you to share them with other people, unless they were present with you at that very moment. Most of the internal matters of a company are not to be disclosed with third parties outside the company environment. It follows that executives of any hierarchy level gain credits when they are considered trustworthy.

Tip #48

Do not trust anyone in the workplace completely.

It is most probable that you have not shared a life-altering experience or important life events with anyone in your company, therefore you can never be absolutely certain how they will treat you during critical situations. On the contrary, you probably met people who need to work to support their families, pursue personal aspirations and follow ideas and attitudes which might not always work for your interest. In this respect, it is best to keep some distance and only trust people who appear to have the same values and principles.

Tip #49

Avoid sentimentalism.

However cold this may sound, sentiment is there provided that everything else works well. The moment something disrupts the harmony within the workplace, you must be able to act objectively. In times of crisis where prompt action is vital for the survival of an organisation, objectivity and sound judgement are vital and can raise the status of managers / leaders.

Tip #50

I have kept for the end a very basic but at the same time very hard tip which, if combined with all the previous ones, can protect you from unfortunate situations.

Within any organisation, you will meet people who do their work in an honourable way, but also people who work their way up in the hierarchy by aiming to tarnish their colleagues' reputation.

People might say things about you which are not true or discuss you in the office when you are not there to stand for yourself. The only way you can survive intact from this sort of situations is to have already proved your value within the company. Even if people keep trying to harm you, you will already be indispensable.

In this sense, my last tip is the following: *Focus on your duties and try to perform as efficiently as possible.*

Additional Note

The tips included in this book aim at assisting managers and team leaders execute their duties, make decisions and take steps as efficiently as possible. By all means, sentiment plays an important role in empathising with colleagues or fellow-citizens who experience unfortunate situations and in no way do I intend to suggest that individuals can only be efficient when they get rid of sentimentalism or refuse to seek for support within their work and/or friendly environment. It is probably more accurate to argue that true leadership does not exclude sentiment completely but rather prescribes control over one's feelings.

Acknowledgements

It is often the case that, upon completion of a work, the writer reflects back to how it all started and recollects the circumstances which allowed this venture to come to an end. Working long hours in a highly stressful and frantic environment, in-between phone calls and meetings, even the most important or practical new ideas might slip one's mind. Just think of how many times you happened to have a fit of inspiration and then lose it all at once, simply because there were other important things to be done at that very moment.

Keeping these thoughts in mind, I would like to express my deepest gratitude to all the people who helped me during this and my former writing attempts. These are no other than my friends and colleagues.

Firstly, I would like to thank Filio Sulvatzi who has significantly influenced my decisions during writing this book.

Another one goes to Alexandros Lefkopoulos, for being my silent supporter.

I am also grateful to my colleague, Petros Polis, for sparing some of his free time during August 2013 to help me find practical examples for my research.

Without the help and support of these people, it is highly unlikely that I would have made it to the end, particularly during all these times when I have been so busy with professional and personal affairs.

I am also thankful for their support during my interview to Stu Taylor for his show in *Money Matters radio*, which is being broadcast from Boston and across the United States.

Another person I would like to thank is Christina Katzika, who took the time to give me feedback on my work during her summer holiday.

Moreover, a big 'thank you' goes to my dear colleagues Spiros, Vivi, Dimitra, Vangelis and Ilias, whom, although in Athens, I have met or spoken to almost every day during the past few years.

Besides, I am very grateful to my colleagues in Northern Greece for their support over the years and I admire them for their great accomplishments even in these hard times we are going through.

I would like to thank my two 'technocrat' friends in Kozani, whom I visit almost every month, as well as Nikos Kiousis for his Management insight and all these endless, inspirational conversations.

I also express my sheer gratitude to my dear father and my beloved brother, Panagiotis Baroutas.

The same holds for my mentor A.I.Z.

Last but not least, I would like to thank my wife for her continuous support in all of my ventures and for being such an amazing spouse. My dearest Sofia, thank you so much!

www.ingramcontent.com/pod-product-compliance
Lightning Source LLC
Chambersburg PA
CBHW071747170526
45167CB00003B/976